Charles Dickens

Mr. Nightingale's Diary

A Farce in one Act

Charles Dickens

Mr. Nightingale's Diary
A Farce in one Act

ISBN/EAN: 9783337119058

Printed in Europe, USA, Canada, Australia, Japan

Cover: Foto ©ninafisch / pixelio.de

More available books at **www.hansebooks.com**

Mr. Nightingale's Diary:

A Farce

IN ONE ACT.

By CHARLES DICKENS.

ı

BOSTON:

JAMES R. OSGOOD AND COMPANY,

Late Ticknor & Fields, and Fields, Osgood, & Co.

1877.

First performed at Devonshire House, London, 1851.

DRAMATIS PERSONÆ.

MR. NIGHTINGALE . . . . Mr. Dudley Costello.

MR. GABBLEWIG (*of the Middle Temple*) . . . . " Charles Dickens.

TIP (*his Tiger*) . . . . " Augustus Egg.

SLAP (*professionally Mr. Formiville*) . . . . " Mark Lemon.

LITHERS (*landlord of the Water-Lily*) . . . . " Wilkie Collins.

ROSINA . . . . Miss Ellen Chaplin.

SUSAN . . . . Mrs. Coe.

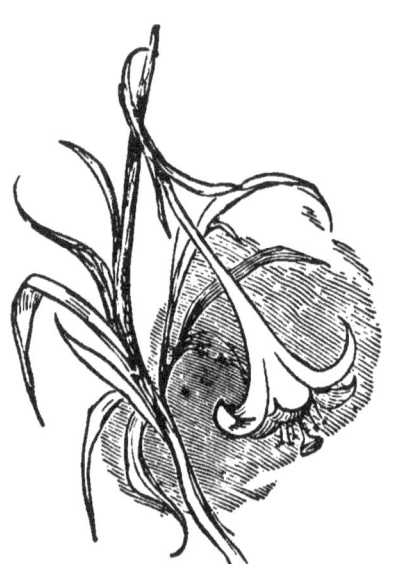

MR. NIGHTINGALE'S DIARY.

SCENE I.

The Common Room of the Water-Lily at Malvern. Door and window in flat. A carriage stops. Door-bell rings violently.

TIP (*without*).

OW, then! Wai-ter! Landlord! Somebody! (*Enters through door, with a quantity of luggage, meeting* LITHERS *running in, L.*)

LITHERS.

Here you are, my boy.

TIP (*much offended*).

My boy! Who are you boying of!

Don't do it. I won't have it. The worm will turn if it 's trod upon.

LITHERS.

I never trod upon you.

TIP.

What do you mean by calling *me* a worm?

LITHERS.

You called yourself one. You ought to know what you are better than I do.

GABBLEWIG (*without*).

Has anybody seen that puppy of mine — answers to the name of "Tip" — with a gold-lace collar? (*Enters.*) O, here you are! You scoundrel, where have you been?

LITHERS.

Good gracious me! Why, if it ain't Mr. Gabblewig, Junior!

GABBLEWIG.

What, Lithers! Do *you* turn up at Malvern Wells, of all the places upon earth?

LITHERS.

Bless you, sir, I 've been landlord of this place these two years! Ever since you did me that great kindness, — ever since you paid out that execution for me when I was in the greengrocery way, and used to wait at your parties in the Temple — which is five years ago come Christmas, — I 've been (through a little legacy my wife dropped into) in the public line. I 'm overjoyed to see you, sir. How do you do, sir? Do you find yourself pretty well, sir?

GABBLEWIG (*moodily seating himself*).

Why, no, I can't say I *am* pretty well.

TIP.

No more ain't I.

GABBLEWIG.

Be so good as to take those boots of
yours into the kitchen, sir.

TIP (*reluctantly*).

Yes, sir.

GABBLEWIG.

And the baggage into my bedroom.

TIP.

Yes, sir. (*Aside.*) Here's a world!

[*Exit, L.*

LITHERS.

The Queen's Counsellor, that is to be,
looks very down, — uncommonly down.
Something's wrong. I wonder what it
is. Can't be debt. Don't look like
drinking. Hope it isn't dice! Ahem!
Beg your pardon, Mr. Gabblewig, but

you 'd wish to dine, sir? He don't hear. (*Gets round, dusting the table as he goes, and at last stoops his head so as to come face to face with him.*) What would you choose for dinner, Mr. Gabblewig?

GABBLEWIG.

O, ah, yes! Give me some cold veal.

LITHERS.

Cold veal! He 's out of his mind.

GABBLEWIG.

I 'm a miserable wretch. I *was* going to be married. I am *not* going to be married. The young lady's uncle refuses to consent. It 's all off — all over — all up!

LITHERS.

But there are other ladies —

GABBLEWIG.

Don't talk nonsense.

LITHERS (*aside*).

All the rest are cold veal, I suppose.
(*Aloud.*)   But, — you 'll excuse my taking the liberty, being so much beholden
to you, — but could n't anything be
done to get over the difficulty?

GABBLEWIG.

Nothing at all.   How is it possible?
Do you know the nature of the uncle's
objection?   But of course you don't.
I 'll tell you.   He says I speak too fast
and *am* too slow, — want reality of purpose, and all that.   He says I 'm all
words.   What the devil else does he
suppose I *can* be, being a lawyer!   He
says I happen to be counsel for his
daughter just now, but after marriage
might be counsel for the opposite side.
He says I am wanting in earnestness, —
deficient in moral go-aheadism.

LITHERS.

In which ?

GABBLEWIG.

Just so. In consequence of which you behold before you a crushed flower. I am shut up and done for — the peace of the valley is fled — I have come down here to see if the cold-water cure will have any effect on a broken heart. Having had a course of wet blanket, I am going to try the wet sheet. Dare say I shall finish erelong with a daisy counterpane.

LITHERS (*aside*).

Everybody 's bit by the cold water. It will be the ruin of our business.

GABBLEWIG.

If the waters of Malvern were the waters of Lethe, I 'd take a douche forty feet high this afternoon, and drink

five-and-twenty tumblers before breakfast to-morrow morning.   Anything to
wash out the tormenting remembrance
of Rosina Nightingale.

LITHERS.

Nightingale, Mr. Gabblewig?

GABBLEWIG.

Nightingale.   As the Shakespeare
duet went in the happy days of our
amateur plays : —

> "The Nightingale alone,
> She, poor bird, as all forlorn,
> Leaned her breast uptil a thorn."

I've no doubt she's doing it at the
present moment, or leaning her head
against the drawing-room window, looking across the Crescent.   It's all the
same.

LITHERS.

The Crescent, Mr. Gabblewig?

GABBLEWIG.

The Crescent.

LITHERS.

Not of Bath?

GABBLEWIG.

Of Bath.

LITHERS (*feeling in his pocket*).

Good gracious!   (*Gives letter.*)   Look at that, sir.

GABBLEWIG.

The cramped hand of the obstinate old bird who might, could, and should have been, and would n't be my uncle-in-law. (*Reads.*) "Christopher Nightingale's compliments to the landlord of the Water-Lily, at Malvern Wells."

LITHERS.

The present establishment.

GABBLEWIG (*reading*).

"And hearing it is a quiet, unpretending, well-conducted house, requests to have the following rooms prepared for him on Tuesday afternoon."

LITHERS.

The present afternoon.

GABBLEWIG (*reading*).

"Namely, a private sitting-room with a" — what? a weed? He don't smoke.

LITHERS (*looking over his shoulder*).

A view, sir.

GABBLEWIG.

Oh! "with a view." Ay, ay. "A bedroom for Christopher N. with a — " what? with a wormy pew?

LITHERS (*looking over his shoulder*).

A warming-pan.

GABBLEWIG.

To be sure; but it's as like one as the other — " with a warming-pan, and two suitable chambers for Miss Rosina Nightingale." — Support me.

LITHERS.

Hold up, Mr. Gabblewig.

GABBLEWIG.

You might knock me down with a feather.

LITHERS.

But you need n't knock me down with a barrister. Hold up, sir.

GABBLEWIG (*reading*).

"And her maid." Christopher Nightingale intends to try the cold-water cure.

LITHERS.

I beg your pardon, sir, what's his complaint?

GABBLEWIG.

Nothing.

LITHERS (*shaking head*).

He'll never get over it, sir. Of all the invalids that come down here, the invalids that have nothing the matter with them are the hopeless cases.

GABBLEWIG (*reading*).

" Cold-water cure, having drunk (see diary) four hundred and sixty-seven gallons, three pints and a half of the various celebrated waters of England and Germany, and proved them to be all Humbugs. He has likewise proved (see diary) all Pills to be Humbugs. Miss Rosina Nightingale, being rather low, will also try the cold-water cure, which will probably rouse her." — Never.

" Perhaps she, like me, may struggle with — "

And I have no doubt of it, Lithers, for she has the tenderest heart in the world —

"Some feeling of regret,"

Awakened by the present individual.

"But if she lov'd as I have lov'd,"

And I have no doubt she did and does,

"She never can forget."

And she won't, I feel convinced, if it's only in obstinacy. (*Gives back letter.*)

LITHERS.

Well, sir, what'll you do? I'm entirely devoted to you and ready to serve you in any way. Will you have a ladder from the builders, and run away with the young lady in the middle of the night, or would the key of the street door be equally agreeable?

GABBLEWIG.

Neither. Can't be done. If it could be done I should have done it at Bath. Grateful duty won't admit of union without consent of uncle — uncle won't give consent — stick won't beat dog — dog won't bite pig — pig won't go over the stile — and so the lovers will never be married (*sitting down as before*). Give me the cold veal, and the day before yesterday's paper. (*Exit* LITHERS *and returns immediately with papers.*)

SLAP (*without*).

Halloo, here. My name is Formiville. Is Mr. Formiville's luggage arrived? Several boxes were sent on beforehand for Mr. Formiville; are those boxes here? (*Entering at door, preceded by* LITHERS, *who bows him in.*) Do you hear me, my man? Has Mr.

Formiville's luggage — I am Mr. Formiville — arrived?

LITHERS.

Quite safely, sir, yesterday.   Three
boxes, sir, and a pair of foils.

SLAP.

And a pair of foils.   The same.
Very good.   Take this cap.   (LITHERS
puts it down.)   Good.   Put these gloves
in the cap (LITHERS *does so*).   Good.
Give me the cap again, it's cold (*he
does so*).   Very good.   Are you the
landlord?

LITHERS.

I am Thomas Lithers, the landlord,
sir.

SLAP.

Very good.   You write in the title-
pages of all your books, no doubt,

"Thomas Lithers is my name
And landlord is my station,
Malvern Wells my dwelling-place,
And chalk my occupation."

What have you got to eat, my man!

LITHERS.

Well, sir, we could do you a nice steak, or we could toss you up a cutlet, or —

SLAP.

What have you ready dressed, my man?

LITHERS.

We have a very fine York ham, and a beautiful fowl, sir —

SLAP.

Produce them! Let the banquet be served — stay, have you —

LITHERS (*rubbing hands*).

Well, sir, we have, and I can strongly recommend it.

SLAP.

To what may that remark refer, my friend?

LITHERS.

I thought you mentioned Rhine wine, sir.

SLAP.

O truly, yes, I think I did.   Yes, I'm sure I did.   Is it very fine?

LITHERS.

It's uncommon fine, sir.   Liebfraumilch of the most delicious quality.

SLAP.

You may produce a flask.   The price is no consideration, (*aside*) as I shall never pay for it.

LITHERS.

Directly, sir.   [*Exit.*

SLAP.

So. He bites. He will be done.
If he *will* be done he *must* be done.
I can't help it. Thus men rush upon
their fate. A stranger! Hum! Your
servant, sir. My name is Formiville —

GABBLEWIG (*who has previously observed him*).

Of several provincial theatres, I believe, and formerly engaged to assist an
amateur company at Bath, under the
management of —

SLAP (*with a theatrical pretence of being affected*).

Mr. Gabblewig! Heavens! This
recognition is so sudden, so unlooked-
for — it unmans me. (*Aside.*) Owe
him £ 15, four shirts, and a waistcoat.
Hope he's forgotten the loan of those
trifles. — O sir, if I drop a tear upon
that hand —

GABBLEWIG.

Consider it done. Suppose the tear, as we used to say at rehearsal. How are you going on? You have left the profession?

SLAP (*aside*).

Or the profession left me. I either turned it off, or it turned me off; all one. (*Aloud.*) Yes, Mr. Gabblewig, I am now living on a little property — that is, have expectations — (*aside*) of doing an old gentleman.

GABBLEWIG.

I have my apprehensions, Mr. Formiville, otherwise, I believe, Mr. Slap —

SLAP.

Slap, sir, was my father's name. Do not reproach me with the misfortunes of my ancestors.

GABBLEWIG.

I was about to say, Slap, otherwise Formiville, that I have a very strong belief that you have been for some time established in the begging-letter-writing business. And when a gentleman of that description drops a tear on my hand, my hand has a tendency to drop itself on his nose.

SLAP.

I don't understand you, sir.

GABBLEWIG.

I see you don't. Now the danger is that I, Gabblewig, may take the profession of the law into my own hands, and eject Slap, otherwise Formiville, from the nearest casement or window, being at a height from the ground not exceeding five-and-twenty feet.

SLAP (*angrily*).

Sir, I perceive how it is. A vindictive old person of the name of Nightingale, who denounced me to the Mendicity Society, and who has pursued me in various ways, has prejudiced your mind somehow, publicly or privately, against an injured and calumniated victim. But let that Nightingale beware. For, if the Nightingale is not a bird, though an old one, that I will catch yet once again with chaff, and clip the wings of, too, I'm — (*aside*) Confound my temper, where's it running? (*Affects to weep in silence.*)

GABBLEWIG (*aside*).

Oho! That's what brings him here, is it! A trap for the Nightingales! I may show the old fellow that I have some purpose in me, after all. Those

amateur dresses among my baggage —
Lithers's assistance — done.   Mr. Formiville.

SLAP (*with injured dignity*).

Sir ?

GABBLEWIG (*taking up hat and stick*).

As I am not ambitious of the honor
of your company, I shall leave you in
possession of this apartment.   I believe
that you are rather absent, are you not ?

SLAP.

Sir, I am, rather so.

GABBLEWIG.

Exactly.   Then you will do me the
favor to observe that the spoons and
forks of this establishment are the private property of the landlord.   [*Exit.*

SLAP.

And that man wallows in eight hundred a year; and half that sum would

make my wife and children, if I had any, happy. (*Enter* LITHERS *with tray on which are fowl, ham, bread, and glasses.*) But arise, black vengeance, Nightingale shall suffer doubly. Nightingale found me out. When a man finds me out in imposing on him, I never forgive him, and when he don't find me out, I never leave off imposing on him. Those are my principles. What, ho! Wine here!

LITHERS (*arranging table and chair*).

Wine coming, sir, directly. My young man has gone below for it. (*Bell without.*) More company! Mr. Nightingale, beyond a doubt. (*Showing him in at door.*) This way, sir, if you please. Your letter received, sir, and your rooms prepared.

SLAP (*looking off melodramatically before seating himself at table*).

Is that the malignant whom these

eyes have never yet betasted with a look? Caitiff, tremble!

Sits as NIGHTINGALE *enters with* ROSINA *and* SUSAN. NIGHTINGALE *muffled in a shawl and carrying a great-coat.*

NIGHTINGALE (*to* LITHERS).

That'll do, that'll do. Don't bother, sir. I'm nervous, and can't bear to be bothered. What I want is peace. Instead of peace, I've got (*looking at* ROSINA) what rhymes to it, and isn't at all like it. (*Sits, covering his legs with his great-coat.*)

ROSINA.

O uncle, is it not enough that I am never to redeem those pledges which —

NIGHTINGALE.

Don't talk to me of redeeming pledges, as if I was a pawnbroker — Oh! (*starts*).

ROSINA.

Are you ill, sir?

NIGHTINGALE.

Am I ever anything else, ma'am? Here. Refer to my diary (*gives book*), Rosina; save me the trouble of my glasses. See last Tuesday.

ROSINA.

I see it, sir (*turning over leaves*).

NIGHTINGALE.

What's the afternoon entry?

ROSINA (*reads*).

New symptom. Crick in back. Sensation as if Self a stiff bootjack suddenly tried to be doubled up by strong person.

NIGHTINGALE (*starts again*).

Oh!

ROSINA.

Symptom repeated, sir?

NIGHTINGALE.

Symptom repeated. I must put it down. (SUSAN *brings chair and produces screw inkstand and pen from her pocket.* NIGHTINGALE *takes the book on his knee and writes.*) Symptom repeated — Oh ! (*Starts again.*) Symptom repeated (*Writes again.*) Mr. Lithers, I believe.

LITHERS.

At your service, sir.

NIGHTINGALE.

Mr. Lithers, I am a nervous man, and require peace. We had better come to an understanding. I am a water patient, but I 'll pay for wine. You 'll be so good as to call the pump sherry at lunch, port at dinner, and brandy and water at night. Now be so kind as to direct the chambermaid to show this discontented young lady her room.

LITHERS.

Certainly, sir. This way, if you please, miss. (*He whispers her ; she screams.*)

NIGHTINGALE (*alarmed*).

What 's the matter ?

ROSINA.

O uncle ! I felt as if — don't be frightened, uncle — as if something had touched me here (*hand on heart*) so unexpectedly that I — don't be frightened, uncle — that I almost dropped, uncle.

NIGHTINGALE.

Lord bless me ! Bootjack and strong person contagious ! Susan, a mouthful of ink. (*Dips his pen in her inkstand and writes.*) Symptom shortly afterwards repeated in niece. Susan, *you* don't feel anything particular, do you ?

SUSAN.

Nothing whatever, sir.

NIGHTINGALE.

You never do. You are the most aggravating young person in the world.

SUSAN.

Lor, sir, you would n't wish a party ill, I 'm sure.

NIGHTINGALE.

Ill! you are ill, if you only knew it. If you were as intimate with your own interior as I am with mine, your hair would stand on end.

SUSAN.

Then I 'm very glad of my ignorance, sir, for I wish it to keep in curl. Now, Miss Rosina. (*Exit* ROSINA, *making a sign of secrecy to* LITHERS, *who goes before.*) Oho! there 's something in the wind that 's not the bootjack.   [*Exit.*

NIGHTINGALE (*seated*).

There's a man yonder eating his dinner as if he enjoyed it. I should say from his figure that he generally *did* enjoy his dinner. I wish I did. I wonder whether there is anything that would do me good. I have tried hot water, and hot mud, and hot vapor, and have imbibed all sorts of springs from zero to boiling, and have gone completely through the pharmacopœia, yet I don't find myself a bit better. My diary is my only comfort (*putting it into his great-coat, unconsciously drops it*). When I began to book my symptoms, and to refer back of an evening, then I began to find out my true condition. Oh! (*Starts.*) That's a new symptom. Lord bless me ! Sensation as if a small train of gunpowder sprinkled from left hip to ankle, and exploded by successful

Guy Fawkes.   I must book it at once,
or I shall be taken with something else
before it's entered.   Susan, another
mouthful of ink !   Most extraordinary !

[Exit.

SLAP *cautiously approaches the diary; as he
does so* GABBLEWIG *looks in and listens.*

SLAP.

What's this ? hum !   A diary — remarkable passion for pills, and quite a
furor for doctors — Very unconjugal
allusions to Mrs. Nightingale.   Poor
Maria! most valuable of sisters ; to me
an annuity, to your husband a torment-
or.   Hum ! shall I bleed him ? meta-
phorically bleed him.   Why not ?   He
never regarded the claims of kindred,
why should I ?   He returns (*puts down
book*).

Re-enter NIGHTINGALE, *looking about.*

NIGHTINGALE.

Bless my heart, I 've left my diary somewhere! O, here is the precious volume, no doubt where I dropped it (*picks up book*). If the stranger had opened it, what information he might have acquired. He 'd have found in it, by analogy, things concerning himself that he little dreams of. He has no idea how ill he is, or how thin he ought to be.   [*Exit.*

SLAP.

Now, then (*tucking up wristbands*), for the fowl in earnest. Where is that wine? Hallo, where is that wine?

Enter GABBLEWIG *as* BOOTS.

GABBLEWIG.

Here you are, sir. (*Starting.*) What do I behold! Mr. Formiville! the imminent tragedian!

SLAP.

Who the devil are you ?   Keep off !

GABBLEWIG.

What ! don't you remember me, sir ?

SLAP.

No.   I don't indeed.

GABBLEWIG.

Not wen I carried a banner with a
silver dragon on it, when you played
the Tartar prince at What 's-his-name's?
and wen you used to bring the house
down with that there pint about re-
wenge, you know ?

SLAP.

What !   Do you mean when I struck
the attitude, and said — Ar-recreant !
The Per-rincess and r-r-revenge are both
my own !   She is my per-risoner —
Tercemble !

GABBLEWIG.

Never! this is to decide. (*They go through the motions of a broadsword combat.* SLAP *having been run through the body sits down and begins to eat voraciously.* GABBLE- WIG, *who has kept the bottle all the while sits opposite to him at table.*) Ah, lor bless me, what an actor you was! (*Drinks.*) That's what I call the true tragic fire, when you strike it out of the swords. Give me showers of sparks, and then I know what you are up to. Lor bless me, the way I've seen you perspire! I shall never see such a actor agin.

SLAP (*complacently*).

I think you remember me.

GABBLEWIG.

Think! Why don't you remember when you left Taunton without paying that there washerwoman, and wen she—

SLAP.

You need n't proceed, it 's quite clear you remember me.

GABBLEWIG (*drinks again*).

Lor bless your heart, yes, what a actor you was! What a Romeo you was, you know! (*Drinks again.*)

SLAP.

I believe there was something in me, as Romeo.

GABBLEWIG.

Ah, and something of you too. The Montagues was a fine family when you was the lightest weight among 'em. And lor bless my soul, what a Prince Henry you was! I see you a drinking the sack now, I do (*drinks again*).

SLAP.

I beg your pardon, my friend, is that my wine?

GABBLEWIG (*affecting to meditate and drinking again*).

Lor bless me, what a actor! I seem to go into a trance like when I think of it. (*Is filling his glass again when* SLAP *comes round and takes the bottle.*) I'll give you Formiville and the Draymer! Hooray! (*Drinks, and then takes a leg of the fowl in his fingers;* SLAP *removes the dish.*)

SLAP (*aside*).

At least he does n't know that I was turned out of the company in disgrace. That's something. Are you the waiter here, my cool but discriminative acquaintance?

GABBLEWIG.

Well, I'm a sort of waiter and a sort of half-boots. I was with a Travelling Circus arter I left you. The riders! the riders! Be in time, be in time. Now, Mr. Merryman, all in to begin.

All that you know. But I shall never see acting no more. It went right out with you, bless you! (*All through this dialogue whenever* SLAP *in a moment of confidence replaces the fowl or wine* GABBLEWIG *helps himself.*)

SLAP (*aside*).

I'll pump him — rule in life. Whenever no other work on hand, pump. (*To him.*) I forget your name.

GABBLEWIG.

Bit, Charley Bit. That's my real name. When I first went on with the banners I was Blitheringtonfordbury. But they said it came so expensive in the printing that I left it off.

SLAP.

Much business done in this house?

GABBLEWIG.

Wery flat!

SLAP.

Old gentleman in nankeen trousers been here long?

GABBLEWIG.

Just come. What do you think I've heard? S'posed to be a bachelor, but got a wife.

SLAP.

No!

GABBLEWIG.

Yes.

SLAP.

Got a wife, eh! ha, ha, ha! You're as sharp as a lancet. Ha, ha, ha! Yes, yes, no doubt. Got a wife. Yes, yes.

GABBLEWIG (aside).

Eh! A flash! The intense enjoyment of my friend suggests to me that old Nightingale has n't got a wife; that he's free but does n't know it. Fraud.

Mum. (*To him.*) I say you're a — but Lor bless my soul, wot a actor you was!

SLAP.

It's really touching, his relapsing into that! But I can't indulge him, poor fellow! My time is precious. You were going to say —

GABBLEWIG.

I was going to say you are up to a thing or two, and so — but, Lor bless my heart alive, what a Richard Third you was! Wen you used to come the sliding business, you know — (*both starting up and doing it*).

SLAP.

This child of nature positively has judgment. It *was* one of my effects. Calm yourself, my good fellow. And so you were observing —

GABBLEWIG (*close to him in a sudden whisper.*)

And so I'll tell you. He hasn't really got a wife. She's dead. (SLAP *starts.* GABBLEWIG *aside.*) I'm right. He knows it. Mrs. Nightingale's as dead as a door nail.

A pause; they stand close together looking at each other.

SLAP.

Indeed! (GABBLEWIG *nods.*) Some piece of cunning, I suppose. (GABBLEWIG *winks.*) Buried somewhere, of course? (GABBLE-WIG *lays his fingers on his nose.*) Where? (GABBLEWIG *looks disconcerted.*) All's safe. No proof. (*Aloud.*) Take away.

GABBLEWIG (*as he goes to table*).

Too sudden on my part. Formiville wins first knock-down blow. Never mind. Gabblewig, up again and at him once more. (*Clears table and takes away tray.*)

SLAP.

How does he know? He's in the market. Shall I buy him? Not yet. Necessity not proved. With Nightingale here, and my dramatic trunks up stairs, I'll strike at least another blow on the hot iron for myself, before I think of taking a partner into the forge.

[*Exit.*

As GABBLEWIG *returns, enter* SUSAN.

GABBLEWIG.

Susan, Susan!

SUSAN.

Susan, indeed! Well, diffidence ain't the prevailing complaint at Malvern!

GABBLEWIG.

Don't you know me? Mr. Gabble —

SUSAN.

Wig! Why, la, sir, then *you*'re the bootjack. Now I understand, of course.

GABBLEWIG.

More than I do! I the bootjack! Susan, listen. Did you know that Mr. Nightingale had been married?

SUSAN.

Why, I never heard it exactly.

GABBLEWIG.

But you 've seen it, perhaps; had a peep into that eternal diary, eh?

SUSAN.

Well, sir, to say the pious truth, I did read one day something or another about a — a wife. You see he married a wife when he was very young.

GABBLEWIG.

Yes.

SUSAN.

And she was the plague of his life ever afterwards.

GABBLEWIG.

O, Rosina, can such things be? Yes. Susan, I think you are a native of Malvern.

SUSAN.

Yes, sir, leastways I was so before I went to London.

GABBLEWIG.

You persuaded Mr. Nightingale to come down here in order that he might try the water-cure.

SUSAN.

La, sir.

GABBLEWIG.

And in order that you might see your relations.

SUSAN.

La, sir, how did you know that?

GABBLEWIG.

Knowledge of human nature, Susan. Now rub up your memory and tell me, did you ever know a Mrs. Nightingale who lived down here? Think — your eyes brighten, you smile, you did know a Mrs. Nightingale who lived down here.

SUSAN.

To be sure I did, sir, but that could never have been —

GABBLEWIG.

Your master's wife? I suspect she was. She died?

SUSAN.

Yes, sir.

GABBLEWIG.

And was buried —

SUSAN.

You know everything.

GABBLEWIG.

In —

SUSAN.

Why, in Pershore Churchyard; my uncle was sexton there.

GABBLEWIG.

Uncle living?

SUSAN.

Ninety years of age.   With a trumpet —

GABBLEWIG.

That he plays on?

SUSAN.

Plays on?   No.   Hears with.

GABBLEWIG.

Good.   Susan, make it your business to get me a certificate of the old lady's death, and that within an hour.

SUSAN.

Why, sir?

GABBLEWIG.

Susan, I suspect the old lady walks, and I intend to lay her ghost. You ask how?

SUSAN.

No, sir, I did n't.

GABBLEWIG.

You thought it. That you shall know by and by. Here comes the old bird. Fly! (*exit* SUSAN) whilst I reconnoitre the enemy. [*Exit.*

Enter NIGHTINGALE *and* ROSINA.

ROSINA.

My dear uncle, pray, do nothing rash. You are in capital health at present, and who knows what the doctors may make of you?

NIGHTINGALE.

Capital health! I have n't known a day's health these twenty years (*refers to diary*). January 6th, 1834. Pain in right thumb. Query, gout. Send for Blair's pills. Take six. Can't sleep all night; doze about seven (*turns over leaf*). March 12, 1839. Violent cough. Query, damp umbrella, left by church-rates in hall. Try lozenges. Bed at six. Gruel. Tallow nose. Dream of general illumination. March 13th. Miserable. Cold always makes me miserable. Receive a letter from Mrs. Night — hem!

ROSINA.

What did you say, sir?

NIGHTINGALE.

Have the nightmare, my dear. (*Aside.*) Nearly betrayed myself. (*Aloud.*) You hear this, and you talk about capital health to a sufferer like me. (*Enter* SLAP *dressed as a smug physician; he appears to be looking about the room.*) O, my spirits, my spirits! I wonder what water will do for them.

ROSINA.

Why, reduce them, of course. Ah, my dear uncle, I often think I am the cause of your disquietudes. I often think that I ought to marry.

NIGHTINGALE.

Very kind of you, my dear. (*Enter* GABBLEWIG *with a very large tumbler of water.*) O, all right, young man. I had better begin. So you think that you really ought, my love, purely on my account, to marry a magpie, don't you? (GABBLE-WIG *starts and spills water over* NIGHTINGALE.) What are you about?

GABBLEWIG.

I beg pardon, sir. (*Aside to* ROSINA.) Bless you.

ROSINA.

Ah, Gab!—O uncle, don't be frightened — but —

NIGHTINGALE (*about to drink, spills water*).

Return of bootjack and strong person! I declare, I'm taking all this water externally when I ought to —

SLAP (*seizing his hand*).

Rash man, forbear. Drain that chalice, and your life's not worth a bodkin.

NIGHTINGALE.

Dear me, sir, it's only water. I'm merely a pump patient.

GABBLEWIG *and* ROSINA *speak aside hurriedly.*

SLAP.

Persevere, and twelve men of Malvern will sit upon you in less than a week, and, without retiring, will bring in a verdict of "Found drowned."

GABBLEWIG (*aside to* ROSINA).

I have my cue, follow me directly.
I'll bring you another glass, sir, in
quarter of an hour.

[*Exit.* ROSINA *steals after him.*

SLAP.

A most debilitated pulse (*taking away
water*), great want of coagulum — lymphitic to an alarming degree. Stamina
(*strikes him gently*) weak, decidedly weak.

NIGHTINGALE.

Right! Always was, sir. In '48, —
I think it was '48. (*Refers.*) Yes, here it
is. (*Reads.*) Dyspeptic. Feel as if kit-
ten at play within me. Try chalk and
pea-flour.

SLAP.

And grow worse.

NIGHTINGALE.

Astonishing! I did — yes. (*Reads.*)
Fever. Have head shaved.

SLAP.

And grow worse.

NIGHTINGALE.

Amazing! Sir, you read me like a
book. As there appears to be no
dry remedy for my unfortunate case, I
thought I'd try a wet one, and here
I am, at the cold water.

SLAP.

Water, unless in combination with
alcohol, is poison to you. You want
blood. In man there are two kinds of
blood. One in a vessel called a vein,
hence venous blood. The other in
the vessel called artery, hence arterial
blood; the one dark, the other bright.

Now, sir, the crassamentum of your blood is injured by too much water. How shall we thicken it, sir? (*Produces bottle.*) By mustard and milk.

NIGHTINGALE.

Mustard and milk!

SLAP.

Mustard and milk, sir, exhibited with a balsam known only to myself. (*Aside.*) Rum. (*Aloud.*) Single bottles, one guinea. Case of twelve, ten pounds.

NIGHTINGALE.

Mustard and milk! I don't think I ever tried — Eh — yes. (*Opens diary.*) 1836. I recollect I once took — I took — O, ah, — Two quarts of mustard-seed, fasting.

SLAP.

Pish!

NIGHTINGALE.

And you 'd really advise me not to take water?

Enter GABBLEWIG *and* ROSINA *in walking-dresses, thick shoes, etc. They keep walking about during the following.*

GABBLEWIG.

Who says don't take water? Who says so?

NIGHTINGALE.

Why, this gentleman, who is evidently a man of science.

GABBLEWIG.

Psha! Eh, dear! Not take water! Look at us. Look at us, Mr. and Mrs. Poulter. Six months ago I never took water, did I, dear?

ROSINA.

Never.

GABBLEWIG.

Hated it. Always washed in gin and water, and shaved with spirits of wine. Did n't I, dear?

ROSINA.

Always.

GABBLEWIG.

Then what was I ? What were we, I may say, my precious?

ROSINA.

You may.

GABBLEWIG.

A flabby, dabby couple, like a pair of wet leather gloves; no energy, no muscle, no go-ahead. Now you see what we are. O dear! Ten miles before breakfast—home—gallon of water — ten miles more — gallon of water and leg of mutton — ten miles more — gallon of water — In fact, we 're never quiet, are we, dear?

ROSINA.

Never.

GABBLEWIG.

Walk in our sleep sometimes; can't walk enough, that's a fact, eh, dear?

ROSINA.

Yes, dear.

SLAP.

Confound this fellow, he'll spoil all.

NIGHTINGALE.

Well, sir, if you really could pull up for a few minutes, I should be obliged to you..

GABBLEWIG.

Here we are, then; don't keep us long. (*Looks at watch*, ROSINA *does same.*) Say a minute, chronometer time.

NIGHTINGALE.

You must know I'm an invalid.

GABBLEWIG.

Five seconds.

NIGHTINGALE.

Come down here to try the cold-water cure.

GABBLEWIG.

Ten seconds.

NIGHTINGALE.

Dear me, I wish you would n't keep counting the time in that way, it increases my nervousness.

GABBLEWIG.

Can't help it, sir — twenty seconds — go on, sir.

NIGHTINGALE.

Well, sir, this gentleman tells me that my cranerany —

SLAP.

Cras. Crassamentum must not be made too sloppy.

NIGHTINGALE.

And thereby he advises, sir —

GABBLEWIG.

Forty seconds, eh, dear? (*Show watches to each other.*)

ROSINA.

Yes, dear.

NIGHTINGALE.

I wish you would n't — And that he advises me to try mustard and milk, sir.

SLAP.

In combination with a rare balsam known only to myself. One guinea a bottle. Case of twelve, ten pounds.

GABBLEWIG.

Time 's up. (*Walks again.*) My darling, mustard and milk! Eh, dear? Don't we know a case of mustard and milk? Captain Blower, late sixteen stone, now ten and one half, all mustard and milk.

SLAP (*aside*).

Can anybody have tried it?

GABBLEWIG (*to* NIGHTINGALE).

Don't be done; if I see Blower I'll send him to you — can't stop longer, ten miles and a gallon to do before dinner. Leg of mutton and gallon at dinner. Five miles and a wet sheet after dinner. Come, dear.

[*Exeunt.*

NIGHTINGALE.

A very remarkable couple. What do you think now, sir?

SLAP.

Think, sir? I think, sir, that any man who professes to walk ten miles a day is a humbug, sir. I could n't do it.

NIGHTINGALE.

But then the lady —

SLAP.

I grieve to say that I think she is a humbugess. Those people, my dear sir, are sent about as cheerful examples of the effects of cold water. Regularly paid, sir, to waylay new-comers.

NIGHTINGALE.

La, do you think so? Do you think there are people base enough to trade upon human infirmities?

SLAP.

Think so! I know it. There are men base enough to stand between you (*shows bottle*) and perfect health (*shakes bottle*), who would persuade you that perpetual juvenility was dear at one pound one a bottle, and that a green old

old age of one hundred and twenty was not worth ten pounds the case. That perambulating water-cart is such a man.

NIGHTINGALE.

Wretch! What an escape I 've had. My dear doctor — you are a doctor?

SLAP.

D. D. and M. D. and corresponding member of the Mendicity Society.

NIGHTINGALE.

Mendicity!

SLAP.

Medical. (*Aside.*) What a slip!

NIGHTINGALE.

Then I shall be happy to try a bottle to begin with. (*Gives money.*)

SLAP.

Ah, one bottle. (*Gives bottle.*) I 've

confidence in your case; you've none
in mine.   Ah! well!

NIGHTINGALE.

A case be it, then, and I'll pay the
money at once.   Permit me to try a
little of the mixture.   (*Drinks.*)   It's
not very agreeable.   I think I'll make
a note in my diary of my first sensa-
tions.

Enter GABBLEWIG *as a great Invalid,* ROSINA
as an old nurse.

GABBLEWIG (*calling*).

Rosina, quick, your arm.   (*Aloud.*)
I tell you, Mrs. Trusty, I can't walk
any further.

ROSINA.

Now do try, sir; we are not a quarter
of a mile from home.

GABBLEWIG.

A quarter of a mile! Why, that's a day's journey to a man in my condition!

ROSINA.

O dear, what shall I do?

NIGHTINGALE.

You seem very ill, sir?

GABBLEWIG.

Very, sir. I'm a snuff, sir, a mere snuff, flickering before I go out.

ROSINA.

O sir, pray don't die here; try and get home and go out comfortably.

GABBLEWIG.

Did you ever hear of such inhumanity? And yet this woman has lived on board wages at my expense for thirty years.

NIGHTINGALE.

My dear sir, here's a very clever friend of mine who may be of service.

GABBLEWIG.

I fear not, I fear not. I've tried everything.

SLAP.

Perhaps not *every* thing.   Pulse very debilitated, great want of coagulum, lymphitic to an alarming degree, stamina weak, decidedly weak.

GABBLEWIG.

I don't want you to tell me that, sir.

SLAP.

Crassamentum queer, very queer. No hope but in mustard and milk.

GABBLEWIG (*starting up*).

Mustard and milk !

ROSINA.

Mustard and milk !

SLAP (*aside*).

Is this Captain Blower ?

GABBLEWIG (*to* NIGHTINGALE).

Are you too a victim ?   Have you
swallowed any of that man-slaughtering
compound ?

NIGHTINGALE (*alarmed*).

Only a little, a very little.

GABBLEWIG.

How do you feel ?   Dimness of sight,
feebleness of limbs ?

NIGHTINGALE (*alarmed*).

Not at present.

GABBLEWIG.

But you will, sir, you will.   You 'd

never think I once rivalled that person in rotundity.

NIGHTINGALE.

Never.

ROSINA.

But he'll never do it again, he'll never do it again.

GABBLEWIG.

You'd never think that Madame Tussaud wanted to model my leg, and announce it as an extraordinary addition.

NIGHTINGALE.

I certainly should not have thought it.

GABBLEWIG.

She might now put it in the chamber of horrors.   Look at it!

ROSINA.

It's nothing at all out of the flannel, sir?

GABBLEWIG.

All mustard and milk, sir. I 'm
nothing but mustard and milk.

NIGHTINGALE (*seizes* SLAP).

You scoundrel! and to this state you
would have reduced me.

SLAP.

O, this is some trick, sir, some cheat
of the water doctors.

NIGHTINGALE.

Why, you won 't tell me that he 's
intended as a cheerful example of the
effects of cold water?

SLAP.

I never said he was, he 's one of the
failures; but as two of a trade can
never agree, I 'll go somewhere else and
spend your guinea.   [*Exit.*

GABBLEWIG (*in his own voice*).

What a brazen knave! Second knock-down blow to Gabblewig. Betting even. Anybody's battle. Gabblewig came up smiling and at him again.

NIGHTINGALE (*goes up to* GABBLEWIG).

My dear sir, what do I not owe you? (*Shakes hands.*)

GABBLEWIG.

O, don't do that, sir, I shall tumble to pieces like a fantoccini figure if you do. I am only hung together by threads.

NIGHTINGALE.

But let me know the name of my preserver, that I may enter it in my diary.

GABBLEWIG.

Captain Blower, R. N. (NIGHTINGALE *writes.*) I am happy to have rescued you from that quack. I declare the

excitement has done me good. Rosi —
Mrs. Trusty, I think I can walk now.

ROSINA.

That 's right, sir, lean upon me !

GABBLEWIG.

Oh ! Oh !

NIGHTINGALE.

What 's the matter, Captain Blower ?

GABBLEWIG.

That 's the milk, sir.

NIGHTINGALE.

Dear me, Captain Blower !

GABBLEWIG.

And that 's the mustard, sir.

[*Exit with* ROSINA.

NIGHTINGALE.

Really, this will be the most eventful
day in my diary except one, that day

which consigned me to Mrs. Nightingale and twenty years of misery.   I
have n't seen her for nineteen, though
I have periodical reminders that she is
still in the land of the living, in the
shape of quarterly payments of £ 25,
clear of income tax.   Well, I'm used
to it; and so that I never see her face
again I'm content.   I'll go find Rosina and tell her. what has happened.
Quite an escape, I declare.   [*Exit.*

SUSAN (*entering, in bonnet, etc.*).

What a wicked world this is, to be
sure!   Everybody seems to be trying
to do the best they can for themselves,
and, what makes it worse, the complaint
seems to be catching, for I'm sure I
can't help telling Mr. Gabblewig what
a traitor that Tip is.   I hope Mr. Gabblewig won't come in my way and

tempt me. Ah, here he is, and I 'm
sure I shall fall.

Enter GABBLEWIG.

Well, Susan, have you got the certificate?

SUSAN.

No, sir, but uncle has, and he 'll be
here directly. O sir, if you knew what
I 've heard!

GABBLEWIG.

What?

SUSAN.

I 'm sure you 'd give half a sovereign
to hear, I 'm sure you would.

GABBLEWIG.

I 'm sure I should, and there 's the
money.

SUSAN.

Well, sir, your man Tip 's a traitor,
sir, a conspirator, sir. I overheard him
and another planning some deception.

I could n't quite make out what, but I know it 's something to deceive Mr. Nightingale.

GABBLEWIG.

Find out with all speed what this scheme is about, and let me know. Who 's that mountain in petticoats? Slap, or I 'm not Gabblewig.

SUSAN.

And with him Tip, or I 'm not Susan.

GABBLEWIG.

Another flash! I guess it all. Susan, your mistress will instruct you what to do. Vanish, sweet spirit.

[*Exeunt* GABBLEWIG *and* SUSAN.

Enter SLAP *in female attire; he looks cautiously about.*

SLAP.

I hope he 's not gone out. I 've a presentiment that my good luck is deserting me; but before we *do* part company I'll make a bold dash, and secure something to carry on with. Now, Calomel, I mean Mercury, befriend me. (*Rings.*)

Enter LITHERS.

LITHERS.

Did you ring, ma'am?

SLAP.

Yes, young man. I wish to speak with a Mr. Nightingale, an elderly gent, who arrived this morning.

LITHERS.

What name, ma'am?

SLAP.

Name no consequence, say I come from M'ria.

LITHERS.

M'ria?

SLAP.

M'ria, a mutual friend of mine and
Mr. Nightingale's, one he ought not to
be ashamed of.

LITHERS.

Yes, ma'am. (*Aside.*) Mr. Gabble-
wig 's right.   [*Exit.*

SLAP.

M'ria has been dead these twelve
years, during which time my victim has
paid her allowance with commendable
regularity to me, her only surviving
brother.   Ah, I thought that name was
irresistible, and here he is. (*Enter* NIGHT-
INGALE.)   His trepidation is cheering.
He 'll bleed freely ! What a lamb it is.
(*Courtesies as he comes down.*) Your servant, sir.

NIGHTINGALE.

Now don't lose a moment; you say
you come from Maria — what Maria ?

SLAP.

Your M'ria.

NIGHTINGALE.

I am sorry to acknowledge the responsibility.

SLAP.

Ah, sir, that poor creature's much changed, sir.

NIGHTINGALE.

For the worse, of course.

SLAP.

I'm afraid so. No gin now, sir.

NIGHTINGALE.

Then it's brandy.

SLAP.

Lives on it, sir, and breaks more windows than ever. She's heard that you've come down here.

NIGHTINGALE.

So I suppose, by this visit.

SLAP.

She lives about a mile from Malvern.

NIGHTINGALE (*starts*).

What!   I thought she was down in Yorkshire.

SLAP.

Was and is is two different things. She wanted for to come and see you.

NIGHTINGALE.

If she does I'll stop her allowance.

SLAP.

And have her call every day? M'ria's my friend ; but I know that would n't be pleasant.   She'd a proposal to make; so, M'ria, says I, I'll see your lawful husband, as you is, sir, and propose for you.

NIGHTINGALE.

I 'll listen to nothing.

SLAP.

Not if it puts the sad sea waves between you and M'ria forever ?

NIGHTINGALE (*interested*).

Eh ?

SLAP.

You know she 'd a brother, an excellent young man, who went to America ten years ago.

NIGHTINGALE (*takes out diary*).

I know. (*Reads aside.*) 16th May, 1841, sent £ 50 to Mrs. N.'s vagabond brother going to America. Query, to the devil ?

SLAP.

He 's written to M'ria, to say that if you 'll give her £ 200, and she 'll come out, he 'll take care of her forever.

NIGHTINGALE.

Done.   It 's a bargain.

SLAP.

He bites! — and her son for £ 100 more.

NIGHTINGALE.

What son ?

SLAP.

Ah, sir, you don't know your blessings.   Shortly after you and M'ria separated a son was born.   But M'ria, to revenge herself, which was wrong, — O, it was wrong in her, that was, — never let you know it, but sent him to the workus, as a fondling she had received in a basket.

NIGHTINGALE.

I don't believe a word of it.

SLAP.

She said you would n't.   But seeing

is believing, so I've brought the innocent along with me; I've got the pretty here.

NIGHTINGALE.

Here, in your pocket?

SLAP.

No, at the door. (*They rise.*)

NIGHTINGALE.

At the door!

SLAP.

Come in, Christopher. Named after you, sir; for, spite of M'ria's feelings, you divided her heart with Old Tom. (*Enter* TIP *as Charity Boy.*)

NIGHTINGALE.

O nonsense!

SLAP.

Christopher, behold your par. (*Boxes him.*) What do you stand there for like a eight-day clock or a idol, as if pars was found every day?

TIP (*aside*).

Don't you make me nervous. (*Aloud.*)
And is that my par?

SLAP.

Yes, child. Me, who took you from
the month, can vouch for it.

TIP.

O par!

NIGHTINGALE.

Keep off, you young yellow-hammer,
or I'll knock you down. Hark 'e,
ma'am. If you can assure me of the
departure of your friend and this cub,
I will give you the money. For twenty
years I have been haunted by —

Enter GABBLEWIG *as an old woman.*

GABBLEWIG.

Which the blessed innocent has been
invaygled of, and man-trapped, least-

ways boy-trapped, and never no more
will I leave this 'ouse until I find a
parent's 'ope, a mother's pride, and nobody's (as I'm aware on) joy.

NIGHTINGALE *and* SUSAN *place chair.*

SLAP.

What on earth is this?   Who is a
mother's pride and nobody's joy? (*To*
TIP.) You don't mean to say you are?

TIP (*solemnly*).

I'm a horphan. (*Goes up to* GABBLEWIG.)
What are talking about, you old bed-
lam?

GABBLEWIG (*screaming and throwing arms about*
his neck).

O my 'ope! my pride! my son!

TIP (*struggling*).

Your son!

GABBLEWIG (*aside to him*).

If you don't own me for your mother, you villain, on the spot, I'll break every bone in your skin, and have your skin prepared afterwards by the Bermondsey Tanners.

TIP.

My master! (*Aloud.*) My mother! (*They embrace.*)

SLAP.

Are you mad? Am I mad? Are we all mad? (*To* TIP.) Did n't you tell me that whatever I said —

TIP (*aside*).

You said! What is your voice to the voice o' natur? (*Embraces his master again.*)

SLAP.

Natur! natur! ah! (*Screams. Chair brought.*) O you unnatural monster!

Who see your first tooth dawn on a deceitful world?   Who watched you running alone in a go-cart, and tipping over on your precious head upon the paving-stones in the confidence of childhood?   Who give you medicine that reduced you when you was sick, and made you so when you was n't?

GABBLEWIG.

Who?   Me.

SLAP.

You, ma'am?

GABBLEWIG.

Me, ma'am, as is well beknown to all the country round, which the name of this sweetest of babbies as will giv to his own joyful self when blessed in best Whitechapel mixed upon a pincushcon, and mother saved likewise was Abso-

lom. Arter his own parential father as
never, otherwise than through being bad
in liquor, lost a day's work in the wheel-
wright business, which is and was but
limited, Mr. Nightingale, being wheels
of donkey shays and goats, and one was
even drawed by geese for a wager, and
went right into the centre aisle of the
parish church on a Sunday morning on
account of obstinacy of the animals, as
can be certified by Mr. Wigs the beadle,
afore he died of drawing on his Wel-
lington boots, to which he was not
accustomed, arter a hearty meal of beef
and walnuts, to which he was too par-
shal, and in the marble fountain of that
church this preciousest of infants was
made Absolom, which never can be un-
made no more I am proud to say, to
please nor give offence to no one no-
wheres and nohows.

SLAP.

Would you forswear your blessed
mother M'ria Nightingale, lawful wed-
ded wife of this excellent old gent?
Why don't the voice o' natur claim its
par?

NIGHTINGALE.

O, don't make me a consideration on
any account.

GABBLEWIG.

M'ria Nightingale, which affliction
sore long time she bore —

NIGHTINGALE.

And so did I.

GABBLEWIG.

Physicians was in vain — which she
never had none particklar as I knows
of, exceptin one which she tore his hair
by handfuls out in consequence of dif-
ferences of opinion relative to her com-

plaint; but it was written on her tomb-
stone ten year and more ago, and dead
she is as the hosts of the Egyptian
Fairies.

NIGHTINGALE.

Dead? Prove it, and I'll give you
£50.

SLAP.

Prove it! I defies her. (*Aside.*) I'm
done.

GABBLEWIG.

Prove it! which I can and will directly minit, by my brother the sexton,
as I will produce in the twinkling of
a star or human eye. (*Aside.*) From
this period of the contest Gabblewig
had it all his own way, and went in and
won. No money was laid out, at any
price, on Formiville. Fifty to one on
Gabblewig freely offered, and no takers.

[*Exit.*

SLAP (*aside*).

I don't like this, so exit Slap.

NIGHTINGALE (*seizing him.*)

No, ma'am, you don't leave this place until the mystery is cleared up.

SLAP.

Unhand me, monster, I claims my habeas corpus. (*Breaks from him.* NIGHT-INGALE *goes to the door and prepares to defend the pass with a chair. To* TIP.) As for you, traitor, though I 'm not pugnacious, I 'll give you a lesson in the art of self-defence you shall remember as long as you live.

TIP.

You! the bottle imp as has been my ruin! Reduce yourself to my weight and I 'll fight you for a pound. (*Squares.*)

GABBLEWIG (*without*).

I 'll soon satisfy this gentleman.

SLAP.

Then I'm done, very much done!
I see nothing before me but premature
incarceration, and an old age of gruel.

GABBLEWIG *enters as sexton.*

NIGHTINGALE.

He's very old. My invaluable cen-
tenarian, will you allow me to inquire —

GABBLEWIG.

I don't hear.

NIGHTINGALE.

He's very deaf. (*Aloud.*) Will you
allow me to inquire —

GABBLEWIG.

It's no use whispering to me, sir,
I'm hard of hearing.

NIGHTINGALE.

He's very provoking.   (*Louder.*)
Whether you ever buried —

GABBLEWIG.

Brewed? Yes, yes, I brewed — that is, me and my wife, as has been dead and gone this forty year next hop-picking. My wife was a Kentish woman — we brewed, especially one year, the strongest beer you ever drunk. It was called in our country Samson with his hair on, alluding to its great strength, you understand. And my wife, she said —

NIGHTINGALE (*very loud*).

Buried, not brewed.

GABBLEWIG.

Buried? O, ah! Yes, yes, buried a many. They was strong, too, once.

NIGHTINGALE.

Did you ever bury a Mrs. Nightingale?

GABBLEWIG.

Ever bury a nightingale? No, no, only Christians.

NIGHTINGALE (*in his ear*).

Missis — Mis-sis Nightingale.

GABBLEWIG.

O yes, yes. Buried her — rather a fine woman — married, as the folks told me, an uncommon ugly man. Yes, yes. Used to live here. Here (*taking out pocket-book*), is the certificate of her burial. (*Gives it.*) I got it for my sister. O yes. Buried her. I thought you meant a nightingale. Ha, ha, ha!

NIGHTINGALE.

My dear friend, there's a guinea, and it's cheap for the money. (*Gives it.*)

GABBLEWIG.

I thank 'e, sir, I thank 'e. (*Aside.*)

Formiville heavily grassed, and 1,000
to 1 on Gabblewig.   [*Exit.*

NIGHTINGALE (*after reading certificate*).

You — you inexpressible swindler.
If you were not a woman, I 'd have you
ducked in the horse-pond.

TIP (*on knees*).

O sir, do it, he deserves it.

NIGHTINGALE.

He ?

TIP.

Yes, sir, she 's a he. He deluded
me with a glass of rum and water and
the promise of a £ 5 note.

NIGHTINGALE (*to* SLAP).

You scoundrel !

SLAP.

Sir, you are welcome to your own

opinion. I am not the first man who has failed in a great endeavor. Napoleon had his Waterloo — Slap has his Malvern. Henceforth I am Nobody. The eagle retires to his rock.

Enter GABBLEWIG *in his own dress.*

GABBLEWIG.

You had better stop here. Be content with plain Slap, discard counterfeit Formiville, and we'll do something for you.

SLAP.

Mr. Gabblewig.   [*Exit.*

GABBLEWIG.

Charley Bit, Mr. Poulter, Captain Blower, respectable female, and deaf sexton all equally at anybody's service.

NIGHTINGALE.

What do I hear?

GABBLEWIG.

Me.

NIGHTINGALE.

And what do I see?

ROSINA (*entering*).

Me! Dear uncle, you would have been imposed upon, and plundered, and made even worse than you ever made yourself, but for —

GABBLEWIG.

Me. My dear Mr. Nightingale, you did think I could do nothing but talk. If you now think I can act — a little — let me come out in a new character. (*Embracing* ROSINA.) Will you?

NIGHTINGALE.

Will I? Take her, Mr. Gabblewig. Stop, though. Ought I to give away what has made me so unhappy? Memorandum — Mrs. Nightingale — see diary. (*Takes out book.*)

GABBLEWIG.

Stop, sir. Don't look. Burn that book and be happy. (*Brings on* SLAP.) Ask your doctor. What do you say, Mustard and Milk?

SLAP.

I say, sir, try me, and when you find me not worth a trial, don't try me any more. As to that gentleman's destroying his diary, sir, my opinion is that he might perhaps refer to it once again.

GABBLEWIG (*to audience.*)

Shall he refer to it once more. (*To* NIGHTINGALE.) Well, I think you may.

Curtain.